Contract Law Made Simple

Withdrawn from Stock
Dublin City Public Libraries

D1344097

CONTRACT LAW
MADE SIMPLE

1st Edition

Vanessa M. Morgan
LLB (Hons), LEC, Barrister, Attorney-at-Law

authorHOUSE®

AuthorHouse™
1663 Liberty Drive
Bloomington, IN 47403
www.authorhouse.com
Phone: 1 (800) 839-8640

© 2015 Vanessa M. Morgan. All rights reserved.

No part of this book may be reproduced, stored in a retrieval system, or transmitted by any means without the written permission of the author.

For permission contact : Email: hochoy_ky@yahoo.com

Book design and layout: Paul Krone
Email: paul@cashewcove.com

Published by AuthorHouse 04/30/2015

ISBN: 978-1-5049-0555-8 (sc)
ISBN: 978-1-5049-0554-1 (e)

Print information available on the last page.

Any people depicted in stock imagery provided by Thinkstock are models, and such images are being used for illustrative purposes only. Certain stock imagery © Thinkstock.

This book is printed on acid-free paper.

Disclaimers:
Contract Law Made Simple is designed to provide information to law students studying for the LLB Degree, Parallegals and students studying A'level Law. Students studying other courses which comprise Contract Law will also find this book helpful. It is also beneficial for individuals desirous of understanding contract law. While best efforts have been used in preparing and compiling this book, the Author and publisher make no representations or warranties of any kind and assume no liabilities of any kind with respect to the accuracy or completeness of the contents. Students studying within the Caribbean region should use additional text for Caribbean cases. This book is intended to be used in conjunction with other sources such as Law reports and case books. The Author presents the law in a readable and accessible form by setting out the general principles of the subject with reference to the leading cases.

Because of the dynamic nature of the Internet, any web addresses or links contained in this book may have changed since publication and may no longer be valid. The views expressed in this work are solely those of the author and do not necessarily reflect the views of the publisher, and the publisher hereby disclaims any responsibility for them.

To my greatest joy,
my husband and children

Contents

List of Cases ix

List of Statutes xi

List of Tables xi

Acknowledgement xiii

Preface. xv

Introduction xvii

1 Nature and Sources of Law 19

2 Making a Contract 25

3 Contractual Terms 37

4 Defects in a Contract .43

5 Discharge of a Contract 53

6 Exemption Clauses 65

7 Remedies for Breach of Contract 73

8 Revision. 79

 • Examination Tips. 79

 • Self Test Questions. 79

List of Cases

Harvey v Facey [1893] AC 552 27

Fisher v Bell [1961] 1 QB 394 27

Partridge v Crittenden [1968] 2 All ER 27

Taylor v Laird [1865] 25 L J Ex 329 28

Carlill v Carbolic Smoke Ball [1892] 1 QB 256 .28

Williams v Cowardine [1833] 4B 621 28

Re Wheelan [1645] 2 EWCA 234 28

Felthouse v Bindley [1863] 142 ER 1037 29

Hyde v Wrench [1840] 3 Beav 334 29

Bradbury v Morgan [1862] 1 H&C 249 29

Manchester Diocesan Council for Education v Commercial
& General Investments Ltd [1970] 1 WLR 241 .30

Tinn v Hoffmann [1873] 29 LT 271 30

Brinkibon v Stahag Stahl [1983] 2 AC 34 30

Henthorn v Fraser [1892] 2 Ch 27 31

Holwell Securities Ltd v Hughes [1974] 1 WLR 155 31

Re London & Northern Bank, ex parte Jones [1990] 1 Ch 220 31

Balfour v Balfour [1919] 2 KB 571 32

Jones v Padavatton [1969] 1 WLR 328 32

Simpkins v Pays [1955] 1 WLR 975 32

Rose & Frank Co. v Crompton Bros Ltd [1925] AC 445 32

Lampleigh v Braithwait [1615] HOB 105 33

Thomas v Thomas [1842] 2 QB 851 34

Re McArdle [1951] Ch 669 33

Price v Easton [1833] 4 B & AD 433 34

Pinnels Case [1602] 5 Co Rep 117a 34

Foakes v Bear [1884] 9 App Cas 605 34

Ecay v Godefrey [1974] 80 LI L Rep 286 39

Schawl v Reade [1913] 2 IR 81 40

L'Estrange v Graucob [1934] 2 KB 394 40

Hutton v Warren [1836] 1 M&N 466 42

Livesley v Rathborne [1982] 1 WLR 45 45

R v Kylsant [1850] 1 All ER 44 45

With v O'Flanagan [1936] Ch 575 46
Leaf v International Galleries [1950] 1 All ER 693 48
Coutourier v Hastie [1856] 5 HL 673 49
Tamplin v James [1916] 2 AC 397 50
Great Peace Ltd v Tsavlinis International Ltd [2001] EWCA Civ 1407 50
Pearce v Brooks [1866] LR 1Ex 213 51
Hughes v Asset Manager Plc [1995] 3 All ER 669 51
Archbold v Spanglett Ltd [1961] 1 All ER 417 51
Cutter v Powell [1756] 6 Term R 320 55
Ritchie v Atkinson [1808] 1 KB 219 55
Bolton v Mahadeva [1972] 2 All ER 1322 56
Hoenig v Issac [1952] 2 All ER 176 56
Robinson v Davison [1871] LR6 Ex 269 58
Taylor v Caldwell [1863] 32 LJ QB 164 58
Krell v Henry [1903] 2 KB 740 58
Herne Bay steam Boat v Hutton [1903] 2 KB 683 58
Metropolitan Water Board v Dick Kerr & Co [1918] AC 119 59
Maritime National Fish v Ocean Trawlers [1935] AC 524 59
Davis Contractors Ltd v Fareham UDC [1956] 2 All ER 145 59
BP (Libya ltd v Hunt (No.2) [1979] 1 WLR 783 .61
Chapleton v Barry UDC [1940] 1 KB 532 66
Thompson v LMS Rly [1930] 1 KB 41 67
Thornton v Shoe Lane Parking [1971] QB 163 67
Olley v Marlborough Court Ltd [1949] 1 All ER 127 67
Spurling v Bradshaw [1956] 2 All ER 121 67
Houghton v Trafalgar Insurance Co [1953] 2 All ER 1409 67
Photo Production Ltd v Securicor Transport Ltd [1980] AC 827 68
R & B Custom Brokers Co. Ltd v
United Dominion Trust Ltd [1988] 1 All ER 847 .71
Jackson v Horizon Holidays Ltd [1975] 1 WLR 1468 74
Cohen v Roche [1927] 1 KB 169 75
Phillis v Lamdin [1949] 2 KB 33 75
Stickney v Keeble [1915] AC 386 76
Walters v Morgan [1861] 2 Cox 369 76
Milward v Earl of Thanet [1801] 5 Ves 720 76
County Ltd v Girozentrale Securities [1996] 3 All ER 77
Victoria Laundry v Newman [1949] 2 KB 528 78
Hadley v Baxendale [1854] 9 Exch 341 78

List of Statutes

Unfair Contract Terms Act 1977. 63
Unfair Terms in Consumer Contract Regulations 1999 63
The Law Reform (Frustrated Contracts) Acts 1943. 59
Sale of Goods Act 1979 42
Supply of Goods And Services Act 1982 42

List of Tables

Table 1	Differences Between Criminal Law and Civil Law 21
Table 2	Identifying Offers 27
Table 3	Intention to Create Legal Relations 32
Table 4	Statements Made During Negotiations 39
Table 5	Validity of Exemption Clauses 68

Acknowledgement

The author expresses sincere gratitude to her husband and friend Stennett Bent for his constant support throughout and for the helpful criticism and comments he provided. Invaluable assistance have also been received from Attorney at Law Thamani Smith who provided grammatical feedback. Thanks to Attorney At Law Maurice Smith for his helpful comments. Thanks are also due to Justice Francis Belle for his constructive feedback. The author wishes to record her gratitude to Paul Krone for his very helpful and dedicated service provided in typing, correcting and presenting the book in a very student friendly manner.

Preface

This book is designed primarily for students studying the LLB programme, A Level Law, Parallegal and students of Business Law. The book is also useful for individuals desirous of understanding Contract Law. This first edition of Contract Law Made Simple is substantially written to cover all areas in Contract Law and at the same time to achieve a greater coherence in the presentation of material. This book covers the syllabus requirements of Contract Law. This book assumes that the reader has no previous knowledge of Contract Law and the starting point is using basic principles and whenever legal terms are used, clear layman explanation is also given.

Students are encouraged to read each chapter once thoroughly and then reread a second time ensuring that they understand what is written in the chapter. To aid understanding of each chapter, students are encouraged to make notes within a file. Research has suggested that the act of writing and collecting notes aids in greater understanding of materials. To assist students with preparation of examination this book includes at the end a chapter past examination questions and the recommended style that students should use to answer the questions.

Vanessa Morgan
March 2015

Introduction

This first edition of "Contract Law Made Simple" provides an indepth knowledge of contract law in natural and ordinary language that law students can easily comprehend. This text covers all topics in Contract Law and provides questions at the end of the book to assist students in their grasps and understanding of the subject. Students are encouraged and advised to attempt the questions to ensure that they comprehend the topic. All answers should be written in the IRAC formula. This is the formula suggested to be used in examinations and coursework by law lecturers and examinations markers alike. IRAC is a structured formula that keep students work logical, focused and easily understood.

Contract Law is a very simple and interesting subject, and my experience of the subject has led me to present this text in a style that all students will be able to understand. I hope you will enjoy my book and wish you all success in your coursework and examinations.

Chapter 1

Nature and Sources of Law

Leabharlanna Poibli Chathair Bhaile Átha Cliath
Dublin City Public Libraries

What is Law?

All law students are keen on defining law during their first day on the law programme, and has come to their own conclusions. Many jurist have provided many and varied definitions of law according to their own perception of law. Law can be defined as a body of principles designed to maintain peace and order within the society. My own helpful definition of law is in line with Salmond who defines law as **"the body of principles recognized and applied by the state for the administration of justice".**

Law is intertwined into every aspect of our lives, and govern our daily activities such as our personal relationship (e.g. laws which bann marriage between relatives) laws which govern working condition (e.g. set the standard for health and safety within the working environment) Law which set the standard of care that we must use in certain situations (e.g. treatment expected of a doctor looking after a patient.

Law within the Caribbean Islands are based on English Law for the most part, and English Law remains, by and large, unwritten. English Law is also governed by judicial precedent, which is the practice of following previous decisions of a superior court. There are a number of ways in which law may be classified but the major classification in law is civil law and public law. Civil Law is commonly referred to as private law.

Public Law is concerned with rules of conduct imposed on individuals by the state and its aim is punishment of the wrongdoer. This comprises several specialist areas such as constitutional law, administrative law and criminal law. Proceedings are started by the state and are heard in the respective courts. Private Law or Civil Law are initiated by private individuals and its aim is compensation for the wronged party.

TABLE 1

Differences Between Criminal Law and Civil Law

Criminal Law	Civil Law
Concerns offences against the State	Disputes between private individuals
Preserve order in the community by punishing offenders	Remedy the wrong suffered
Prosecutor prosecutes a Defendant	Plaintiff sues a Defendant
Action is heard in the Criminal Court. For example, a Magistrates Court	Action is heard in a Civil Court
Prosecutor must prove his case beyond reasonable doubt	Claimant must prove his case on a balance of probabilities
Defendant may be convicted if he is found guilty and acquitted if innocent.	Defendant is liable or not liable
Examples of criminal matters: theft, murder, rape	Examples of civil matters: contract, tort, trust

Source: Keenan & Riches, Business Law, 4th Edition, Pitman Publishing

Sources of Law

The term sources of law can be best defined as the different origins of law. How the law comes into existence, are generally regarded as common law and equity. There are also various legal sources which stipulates the law that must be applied to our everyday life and gives guidance to Judges and Legal minds. Some examples are legislation, judicial precedent, statutes etc. There are also literary sources which stipulates the material in which legal sources are recorded. Some of these sources includes Statutes, CARICOM, and some authoritative textbooks which are indirect sources. We will briefly discuss the various sources listed with particular emphasis on common law and equity.

Common Law

What is common law and how did it come into existence? The term common law is typically used to describe all the unwritten laws in England which were imported to the colonies. Put simply, these laws are not recorded in any one document but are contained in several recorded decisions of Judges. This law originated from the practice of local customs which has been practiced for centuries and dates back to the Norman Conquest in 1066. Prior to this era, there was not a unified system of Law within England. England was divided into Saxon Kingdoms, each with its own laws based on their local customs which was also practiced and administered in the local courts.

Equity

The common law became extremely rigid over a period of time and failed to keep pace with an extremely complex and changing society. By the fifteenth (15th) century a body of rules was developed and applied by the court. This body of rules was referred to as equitable rules and they served to compensate aggrieved complainants where the common law was inadequate. The concept of equity is based on justice and fair play. Common law and equity remains two separate but complementary system of law today. A judge is at liberty to draw upon both set of rules to decide a case.

Legislation

This is law enacted by Parliament. Legislation provides a more rapid and efficient means of effecting such legal changes. Legislation is also useful to simplify the law, ie by consolidating and codifying the law.

Judicial Precedent

This is a means whereby Judges in the superior courts makes a judgment for later courts to follow when similar facts come before them for a solution. Whenever a dispute comes before the court the Judges have a duty to listen to the evidence presented and make a ruling which is binding on the parties (this is known as *res judicata*) and by establishing a legal principle which will bind all future cases, known as *ratio decidendi*. Lower courts are obliged to follow the decision of a superior court provided the decision has not been overruled or reversed. A Judgment is overruled when a superior court states at a later date that the decision in a particular case should not be followed.

Where lower courts must follow the superior court judgment, the precedent is termed binding precedent or *stare decisis*. However, where the courts may follow the previous judgment, the precedent is termed persuasive. Examples of persuasive judgments are overseas judgments, *ratio decidendi* of lower courts and the *obiter dicta* of a judgment. *Obiter dicta* are statements taken into account or things said by the way in the judges reasoning in reaching their decision. They are persuasive only and are not binding.

Chapter 2

Making a Contract

Making a contract is a vital characteristic of our everyday life. A person enters contracts all the time, such as buying goods from the supermarket, shops, stores, travelling by air, land and sea, renting an apartment etc. It is the legal mechanism to ensure justice is done if things go wrong.

What is a Contract:

A contract is an agreement by two or more persons for the provision of goods and services, which is binding.

What ingredients should be included in a contract?

1. The Offer
2. Acceptance
3. Intention to create legal relations
4. Consideration

1.   The Offer

Key Definition: An offer is an expression of willingness by the offeror to contract on specified terms, made with an intention that it will become legally binding if those terms are accepted by the offeree.

NOTE: The party who makes an offer is the offeror.

The party to whom the offer is addressed is the offeror.

G.H. Treitel, The Law of Contract (Sweet & Maxwell, London, 2003)

How Do We Identify Offers?

TABLE 2   **Identifying Offers**

Offer	Invitation to Treat	Request for Information
If the advert is quoted in firm word it will constitute an offer. (eg if it states that the first person to return my lost kitten will get $500.00). Carlill v Carbolic Smoke Balls Limited [1892] QB 256	These are normally advertisements. Partridge v Crittenden [1968] 2 All ER	Statements of intention and statement of price. Harvey v Facey [1893] AC 552
The Defendant placed a newspaper advertisement stating that they would pay £100 to anyone who contracts the increasing epidemic influenza, colds, or any disease caused by taking cold, after having used the ball three times daily for two weeks according to the printed directions supplied with each ball. The Claimant caught flu after using the ball as directed and claimed the sum of £100. The Defendants argued that the advertisement was a mere puff and that, in any case, there was no offer made to any particular person and it was impossible to contract with the whole world.	The Defendant placed an advert in a magazine stating Bramblefinch hens 25¢ each. An attempt to prosecute the Dealer under the Protection of wild Birds Act 1954 was unlawful. The court held that the advert was an invitation.	
Legal Principle arising from Carlills' case is that the Court of Appeal held that the offer in the advert was a unilateral offer to the world at large which was accepted by the Claimant, this unilateral offer waived the need for communication of acceptance prior to a claim being made on the basis of it. The Claimant was entitled to the £100.	Fisher v Bell [1961] 1 QB 394 window display of goods at a shop is an invitation to treat.	

How Do We Communicate Offers?

Offers must be communicated to the offeree before it can be accepted. If services are rendered which fulfill the terms of an offer but are done in ignorance of the actual offer, it would be impossible for the reliance to be placed on the offeror as acceptance of the offer. This means no party can be held liable for an offer to which they are unaware. Taylor v Laird [1865] 25 L J Ex 329. As you would already be aware, an offer need not be directed at a specific person. However, it must be communicated to the offeree before he can accept it. Carlill v Carbolic Smoke Ball [1892] 1 QB 256.

NOTE: As long as the offeree is aware of the words or conduct which constitutes the offer, his motive accepting the offer is irrelevant. In Williams v Cowardine [1833] 4B 621 a reward of £20 was offered for information leading to the arrest and conviction of a murderer. The Claimant knew of the award but offered the information to ease her conscience. The Court held that she was still entitled to the reward of £20.

How Do We Terminate Offers?

- **Rejection**
  This can be described as a refusal of the offer by the offeror.
- **Revocation**
  This refers to the rescinding, annulling or withdrawal of an offer.
- **Lapse of Time**
  An offer will end after the time stated. If no time limit has been stated the offer will come to an end after a reasonable time.
- **Death**
  Where the offeror has died and his death is known to the offeree before acceptance, according to Re Wheelan

[1645] 2 EWCA 234 the offer lapses. If the offeree is ignorant of the offeror's death before acceptance, then acceptance is valid unless the contract is one which involves personal services of the offeror Bradbury v Morgan [1862] 1 H&C 249.

2.   Acceptance

What is acceptance? Acceptance is the unconditional assent to all the terms of the offer, communicated to the offeror by the offeree. G.H. Treitel, The Law of Contract (Sweet & Maxwell) London, 2003, 16. Mere silence is not adequate to constitute acceptance. Felthouse v Bindley [1863] 142 ER 1037. For acceptance to be effective the following criteria must be satisfied.

- The acceptance must be close to, or identical to the terms of the offer. If the offeree introduces a new term that is more favourable to him, the original offer is terminated and   is replaced by a new offer, now termed a counter offer, which the offeror may then accept or reject. In Hyde v Wrench [1840] 3 Beav 334, the Defendant offered a farm to the Claimant for £1000. The Claimant said he would accept it for £950. The Defendant refused it and the Claimant said he would pay him the original asking price of £1000. The Court held that the original offer of £1000 had been terminated by the counter offer so that it is no longer open for acceptance.

- Specified mode of acceptance must be adhered to. In instances where the offeror stipulates a specified mode of acceptance, and makes it clear that only be prescribed method will suffice, such mode must be adhered to by the offeree for acceptance to take place. However, if the offeror does not specify that only prescribed method will suffice and the offeree uses an equally expeditious method to the stipulated one that would be sufficient for acceptance to take place. Manchester Diocesan Council for Education v Commercial & General Investments Ltd [1970] 1 WLR 241 and Tinn v Hoffmann [1873] 29 LT 271.

- Acceptance must be communicated. The general rule is that the contract is only created when acceptance is brought to the attention of the offeror. This is the position of the so-called instantaneous contracts, that is contracts by telephone or face-to-face. Therefore, should acceptance take place by telephone and the line goes dead before the offeree hears what has been said, acceptance would not have taken place, and as a result there would be no contract.

- In instances of non- instantaneous communication where the message reaches the offeror at a later stage, the crucial question to consider is the time that the message is received. This is the case where the mode of communication are telefax, email and telephone (where messages are left on the answering machine). The long standing principle adopted by the courts in these instances as demonstrated in Brinkibon v Stahag Stahl [1983] 2 AC 34, shows that a telex message that was sent outside of office hours should not be considered to be an instantaneous means of communication and therefore acceptance could only be effective when the office is reopened. Lord Wilberforce went further to summarise the situation in relation to modern communications methods by stating that: No universal rule can cover all such cases; they must be resolved by reference to the intention of the parties, by sound business practice and in some cases by a judgment where the risk should lie.

Acceptance By Post

This is an exception to the general rule that acceptance must come to the attention of the offeror before a contract comes into existence. The general postal rule is that a contract is created as soon as the letter of acceptance is posted regardless of whether or not the letter is received by the offeror. (Henthorn v Fraser)

When will the postal rule not apply?

- The postal rule will not apply if it would lead to inconvenience and absurdity. Acceptance by post must be normal, and reasonable. In Holwell Securities Ltd v Hughes [1974] 1 WLR 155, the Defendant made an offer to sell a house to the Plaintiffs and stated that acceptance must be made by notice in writing to the intended vendor. The Plaintiffs posted a letter accepting the offer but it was never received by the Defendant. The Court of Appeal refused to apply the postal rule because it was clear that the Defendant had expected to be notified of acceptance before there could be a contract.
- The postal rule will not apply if the letter is not properly stamped and addressed. Re London & Northern Bank, ex parte Jones [1990] 1 Ch 220.
- The postal rule will not apply to telex, fax machines and emails used by individuals other than the post office.
- The postal rule will not apply if the letter is not properly posted. Therefore, handing a letter to a postman who is not authorized to deliver letters is not posting. (Re London v Northern Bank).

3.   Intention to Create Legal Relations

The Courts have long held the view that not all agreements are meant to create contractual force. The Courts have categorized that in domestic and social Agreements it is presumed that the parties do not intend to create legal relations. Agreements of a Commercial nature will always attract an intention to be legally binding. The presumption can generally be rebutted by express provision in the contract.

TABLE 3   **Intention to Create Legal Relations**

Domestic Agreement	Social Agreement	Commercial Agreement
Husband and Wife Parents and Children	Parties sharing home	Business arrangements
Presumption against intention to be legally bound	Presumption against intention to be legally bound	Presumption to be legally bound
Balfour v Balfour [1919] 2 KB 571 Jones v Padavatton [1969] 1 WLR 328	Simpkins v Pays [1955] 1 WLR 975	Rose & Frank Co. v Crompton Bros Ltd [1925] AC 445

4. Consideration

Consideration is an essential element that is needed to constitute a binding Contract. To constitute an Agreement, each party must give something of value. What each party gives is called consideration. There are many definitions of consideration but the shortest and most to the point is Pollock's, "The price for which a promise is bought". As long as one party has provided consideration, he can take legal action against the other party should the other party refuse to fulfill his side of the bargain.

Rules of Consideration - There are a number of rules governing consideration. In short the following are outlined:

Consideration Must Not Be Past

This simply means that the consideration must have been given at the time of the Agreement and cannot be given before the Agreement was contemplated. Example, If X cleans Y car and once X is finished Y promise to pay X for the service. Should Y refuse to pay, X cannot enforce Y promise as Y did not make the promise in return for X to clean the car. In Re McArdle [1951] Ch 669, Miss McArdle paid for repairs to a house owned by her relatives. After the repairs had been carried out the relatives promised to reimburse her but they never fulfilled such promise. Ms McArdle took legal action, her action failed on the grounds that the reimbursement promised was past consideration.

Realistically, one can consider this principle to be somewhat harsh and it had indeed been criticized and considered to be too harsh. The Courts have however developed some exceptions to this rule as follows:

Exceptions to the rule that consideration must not be past

- The Act must have been done at the promisors request
- The parties must have understood that the act was to be renumerated further by a payment or the conferment of some other benefit and payment.
- The payment, or the conferment of a benefit, must have been legally enforceable had it been promised in advance. Lampleigh v Braithwait [1615] HOB 105

Leabharlanna Poiblí Chathair Bhaile Átha Cliath
Dublin City Public Libraries

Consideration Must Be Sufficient But Need Not Be Adequate

It is clearly established rule that the courts will not enquire in to the value of the consideration. In Thomas v Thomas [1842] 2 QB 851 the court held that the payment of £1 was adequate consideration for the lease of a house.

Consideration must move from the Promisee

The person who wishes to enforce the contract must show that they provided consideration. It is not enough to show that someone else provided consideration. Price v Easton [1833] 4 B & AD 433.

Part Payment of a Debt is not Consideration to Discharge Debt

Part Payment of a Debt is not Consideration for a Promise to Discharge the Entire Debt. This long standing principle is known as the rule in Pinnels Case [1602] 5 Co Rep 117a and was later applied in the case of Foakes v Bear [1884] 9 App Cas 605, in which Mrs Bear had promised to forgo the interest on a judgment debt if Dr Foakes paid off the sum in instalments. It was held that Mrs Bear could still legally pursue him for the interest as he had not given any consideration for the promise.

Exceptions to the part payment rule

Consideration might be provided if the creditor agrees to accept :

- Early payment of a smaller sum.
- Delivery of a chattel of a lower value rather than money.
- Part payment on a due date but at a different place to the convenience of the creditor.

The final exception to Pinnels case is the equitable rule of promissory estoppel or the High Trees Principle. The doctrine provides a means of promise binding, in certain circumstances in the absence of consideration. The principle is that if someone makes a promise, which another person acts on, the promisor is estopped from going back on his promise, even though the other person did not provide consideration.

Chapter 3

Contractual Terms

A contract consists of rights and obligations to be performed by the parties to the contract. These are expressed in the statements made by the parties at the time of making the contract, called Express terms. Other obligations/rights are added automatically into the contract by law, called Implied Terms. In this Chapter, we will examine Express terms and its implications should one party fail to fulfill their obligations. We will then move on to consider implied terms.

Express Terms

These are terms expressed by the parties at the time of negotiating the contract. Some of these terms will be written in the contract and gives rise to contractual effect. However, not all statements or promises made during negotiation will form a part of the contract. Some will be termed "mere puff" (boastful advertising statement). Some of these statements will be termed representations. This is a statement which induces the party to enter into the contract but does not form part of the contract. Other statements will be terms, which form a part of the contract. It must be noted that it is essential to distinguish the above categories of statements as the legal consequences that result differs.

TABLE 4   **Statements Made During Negotiations**

Puffs	Representations	Terms
No liability	Liability	Liability
Puffs are not serious	Need proof of fault	Breach of contract, gives right to take legal action

In deciding whether a statement is a representation or a term, the Courts will take certain factors into consideration as established by case laws. The key deciding factor is the intention of the parties.

Points to Note:

Representation

- A statement is likely to be such if the statement maker asked the other party to verify the accuracy of the statement for himself. Ecay v Godefrey [1974] 80 LI L Rep 286.
- Both parties to the statement have equal knowledge in relation to the subject matter.
- Where there is a lapse in time between the statement and the formation of the contract.

Terms

- Statements made with the intention of preventing the other party from verifying the truth. Ecay v Godefrey [1974] 80 LI L Rep 286.

- Recipient of statement places great reliance on statement made. Schawl v Reade [1913] 2 IR 81.
- Statement maker has specialist knowledge or skill in relation to the subject matter.
- Written statement in a signed contract, parties are bound by it whether or not they have read the document and understood it. L'Estrange v Graucob [1934] 2 KB 394.

Parol Evidence Rule

The general parol evidence rule states that where a contract has been reduced into writing, extrinsic evidence whether oral or written is not admissible to add, vary, or contradict the terms. The Law Commission [1976] recommended that the rule should be abolished, but by 1986, it concluded that it did not stop the courts from admitting extrinsic evidence if this was the intention of the parties. A number of exceptions to the general rule has been developed as follows:

- If the written agreement was not intended to be the whole contract on which the parties had actually agreed, parol evidence is admissible.
- To determine the validity of the contract.
- Parol evidence can be used to show that the contract does not yet operate, or that it has ceased to operate.
- Used to show the capacities in which the parties contracted.
- Used to explain words or phrases that are ambiguous , or which if taken literally does not make sense.
- Used to show that the parties made two related contracts, ie collateral contracts.

How Terms are Classified

As stated previously, not all statements included into a contract will be terms. Those that are classed as terms fall into three different categories.

1. **Conditions**: goes to the root of the contract and is the most important term of the contract.
2. **Warranties**: contractual term of lesser importance than condition.
3. **Innominate terms**: concept used by the courts and whose classification is determined once the effects of the breach are known.

It is essential to distinguish between these three types, as breach of these terms have different legal remedies.

Terms

1. **Conditions**: Breach of a condition entitles the innocent party to repudiate the contract and claim damages.
2. **Warranty**: Breach of a warranty entitles the innocent party to claim damages only.
3. **Innominate Terms**: where there is a breach of an innominate term, the court considers the consequences and then make a decision as to the appropriate remedy.

Implied Terms

As with express terms which forms part of a contract, other terms are incorporated into a contract known as implied terms. These terms are formed into the contract in one of the following ways:

- By custom
- By statute
- As fact
- At common law

1. Terms implied by Custom - The courts may admit evidence of known usage or custom. Hutton v Warren [1836] 1 M&N 466.

2. Terms implied by Statute - In some types of contracts, terms will be implied by statute. For example, the sale of goods contract, terms will be implied by the Sale of Goods Act 1979. The supply of goods and services act 1982 deals with contracts for the supply of services and covers two types of services contract, where the supplier provides goods and services and where the supplier provides pure service. This is not an exhaustive list.

3. Terms implied as Fact - The Courts may imply a term into the contract even though there is an absence of expression by the parties. In instances where this is implied by the Court, they take the view that the parties must have intended its inclusion to give the contract business efficacy. This mode of implication is sometimes known as the **Doctrine of the Moorcock.**

4. Terms implied at Common Law - contracts that are of a common occurrence normally falls within this category. In instances where the courts imply a term into a contract for the first time, the same term will be implied into future contracts unless the parties expressly exclude it. These types of contracts are normally contracts between seller and buyer, employer and employee.

Chapter 4

Defects in a Contract

There are many and varied different factors that many times cause a contract to become invalid. This is very common in our society. Although a contract may be perfectly formed, having all the contractual elements, such as offer, acceptance, consideration and legal relations, it may prove unenforceable due to other factors known as vitiating factors. These factors, if known to the parties or either of the party would have prevented the formation of the contract. Some defects such as untrue statements which induce a contract, mistake about the type of contract formed and pressure or force to induce the contract all affect contractual consent.

The consequences for the party vary depending on the gravity of the defect and results in the contract being termed "void", "voidable", "unenforceable" or illegal. This chapter considers the nature and effect of the vitiating factors and will consider misrepresentation first.

Misrepresentation

Misrepresentation can be defined as a false statement of fact made prior or during the formation of the contract that induces one party to enter into the contract. You will notice that there are a number of ingredients within the definition that must be explored further. The following ingredients will be considered:

- False statement
- Fact
- Induce

False Statement

A false statement can be fraudulent, negligent or innocent. These consequences will be discussed later as the degree of falsity is relevant when considering the remedies that are available.

Statement

Statements may be oral or written. Conduct may be sufficient to quality as in Livesley v Rathborne [1982] 1 WLR 45. However, as a general rule mere silence does not constitute misrepresentation. However, there are exceptions to this general rule as follows:

1. **Half Truth** - This is where not all information is disclosed. The undisclosed part would have detrimental effect on the contract which the party who is failing to disclose is aware of. In R v Kylsant [1850] 1 All ER 44, a company gave a misleading impression to would-be investors that it was trading profitably during the depression years. It stated in a prospectus that it had paid a regular dividend during those years, but failed to disclose that it was only able to do so on its accumulated profits.

2. **Fiduciary relationship** - One party may be under a fiduciary duty to disclose information for the benefit of the other. Fiduciary duty arises in relationships such as principal and agent, employer and employee.

3. **Change in circumstances** - The law imposes a duty to correct a statement which was true when made but subsequently becomes untrue at the time the contract is entered into. Case which illustrates this point is With v O'Flanagan [1936] Ch 575, where a statement about the fee income of a medical practice for sale was true when made but became false by the time the signing of the contract took place as the income had fallen due to the sellers illness.

Fact

Misrepresentation must relate to an existing fact. It excludes sales talk, statements of law and statements of future intention. Sales talk is also referred to as "puff", the courts treat such talk as idle boast and attach no contractual importance. An example would be a statement such as "my car is the fastest car in the city".

Induce

The receiver of the statement must have relied on the statement of the other party to enter into the contract. No consequences will lie if the receiver of the statement relied on his own skill and judgment in entering into the contract.

Types of Misrepresentation

Negligent Misrepresentation

This is less serious than fraudulent misrepresentation but more serious than innocent misrepresentation. This is where the statement maker makes a statement carelessly without verifying the accuracy of the statement.

Innocent Misrepresentation

Statement made in the belief that it is true and that there are reasonable grounds for such belief.

Fraudulent Misrepresentation

Most serious type of misrepresentation. Statement made with the knowledge that the statement is false.

Remedies for Misrepresentation

The general effect of misrepresentation is to render the contract voidable. This means the misled party can set aside the contract. Damages are assessed according to tort rules and not contract. Tort rules aim to put the wronged party in the position prior to the misrepresentation. Consequential loss or foreseeable loss, that is loss of profit are recoverable in contract. Additionally, there are other remedies available to the misled party as follows:

Damages - The misled party can recover damages from the statement maker as of right if he has suffered loss and the misrepresentation was fraudulent or negligent. The former is brought in the tort of deceit, while the latter, the action is brought either in the tort of negligence or under the Misrepresentation Act 1967.

Rescind the Contract - The misled party may cancel the contract if performance has not yet taken place. The misled party has no right to rescission if he has affirmed the contract, or if the parties cannot be restored substantially to their pre-contractual position. The courts can use their discretion under section 2 (2) of the Misrepresentation Act 1967 and award damages instead of rescission.

Affirm the Contract - The misled party may affirm the contract, even though fully aware of the misrepresentation, if he decides that the contract is beneficial to him. Failure to exercise a right to cancel the contract within a reasonable time may be evidence of affirmation. Time starts to run against the misled party as soon as the statement is realized. This is the case for fraudulent misrepresentation. With other types of misrepresentation, time starts to run from the date the contract is made and not at the date the statement is discovered. Leaf v International Galleries [1950] 1 All ER 693.

Lapse of time - This may be evidence of affirmation and thus a bar to rescission. This is particularly so where the time lapse before rescission is great. The court determines whether the lapse is great.

Mistake

There is no general doctrine of mistake. Contractually, some situations render a contract void at common law as a result of a mistake made by the parties to the contract. There are three categories of mistake as follows:

- Unilateral mistake
- Common mistake
- Mutual mistake

Unilateral Mistake is typically where one party makes a mistake, and the other knows and takes advantage of the mistake.

Mutual Mistake is where the parties are at cross purposes, but each believes that the other is in agreement.

Common Mistake is where both parties make the same mistake. There is complete agreement between the parties but both are mistaken in regard to a fundamental point as to the existence or quality of the subject matter.

What is the effect of mistake on a contract?

Common Mistake - This type of mistake made as to the existence of the subject matter of the contract is void at common law and equity. Coutourier v Hastie [1856] 5 HL 673. Mistake made as to the quality of the subject matter of the contract is not sufficiently fundamental to be an operative mistake at common law. Leaf v International Galleries [1950] 1 All ER 693.

Unilateral Mistake - This is normally a mistake as to the identity of one of the contracting parties, the terms of the contract or the nature of a signed document. Mistake as to the fundamental character of the contract makes the contract void at common law and in equity. Mistake because of fraud is voidable at common law and equity and mistake of Non est Factum (this is not my act) is void at common law.

Mutual Mistake - This is when the parties do not realize there is a misunderstanding as to the terms of the contract or the subject matter of the contract. The mistake renders a contract void at common law and equity.

Mistake and Equity

As you will recall, we mentioned earlier that the mistake has to be operative to be effective. If the mistake is not operative, equity may be used in any of the following ways:

- Rescission

- Rectification
- Refusal to make order of specific performance

Rescission – The Courts will allow rescission in instances where it is unconscionable to allow one party to take advantage of the mistake. Rescission is not available for a common mistake. Great Peace Ltd v Tsavlinis International Ltd [2001] EWCA Civ 1407.

Rectification - This involves the Courts rectifying documents to conform to the real agreement if there is evidence that the contract does not affect the prior agreement of the parties.

Specific Performance - This is a discretionary remedy. The Courts may refuse to grant it if it would be inequitable to compel that party to perform their contractual obligations or the other party knew of the mistake and took advantage of the mistake. It is important to note that the Court will not withhold an order of specific performance to save the mistaken party from entering into a bad bargain. This was illustrated in Tamplin v James [1916] 2 AC 397.

Illegality

Illegality differs to mistake and misrepresentation to the extent that the latter two concerns whether the contract was entered into voluntarily while the former is concerned with the character of the contract. If a contract is illegal, the illegality may affect the purpose of the contract or the way in which the contract is performed.

Some contracts are rendered illegal by certain statute and common law in that they render some forms of activity illegal.

Contracts rendered illegal at common law are as follows:

- Contracts to promote immorality, Pearce v Brooks [1866] LR 1Ex 213
- Contracts to commit crime or benefit from the proceeds of crime
- Contracts concerning corruption in public life
- Contracts to impede the course of justice
- Contracts in restraint of trade

Contracts rendered illegal by statute:

- Contracts formed for public policy reasons
- Contracts which are formed legally but performed illegally, Hughes v Asset Manager Plc [1995] 3 All ER 669
- Void ab initio, unenforceable

A contract which is wholly illegal on formation is void so that no rights or liabilities can arise. It must be noted that any money or property transferred under an illegal contract cannot be recovered in a court action unless the parties are not equally to be blamed. This situation can arise where one party entered into the contract due to force or fraud. In this situation, the innocent party can obtain recovery. Should a lawfully formed contract be used for an illegal purpose which is known to both parties, the courts will treat the contract as illegal from the onset. Pearce v Brooks [1866] LR 1Ex 213. If one party is unaware of the illegal purpose, then he can enforce the contract. Archbold v Spanglett Ltd [1961] 1 All ER 417.

Chapter 5

Discharge of a Contract

Discharging a contract simply means to bring the contract to an end. This is only possible when the parties have fulfilled their obligations under the contract. However, in some instances, the contract comes to an end before performance of the contract takes place. As we go through this chapter, we will learn the of the following ways in which a contract can come to an end:

- Discharge by Performance;
- Discharge by Agreement;
- Discharge by Breach;
- Discharge by Frustration.

1. Discharge by Performance

Performance of the contract simply means that the parties to the contract have fulfilled their obligations under the contract in the manner articulated in the contract. This rule is related to entire contracts which require complete performance and can give rise to harsh consequences if not adhered to. In Cutter v Powell [1756] 6 Term R 320, a seaman contracted to work on a ship for a complete voyage for 30 guineas. The seaman died mid-voyage. The widow of the seaman failed to recover the money because he had not completed performance of his contractual obligation. (This situation is now covered by the Merchant Shipping Act 1980)

To this somewhat harsh rules are exceptions created by the common law:

- **Acceptance of partial performance** - where partial performance by one party is accepted by the other party, the other is legally entitled to pay for the work done on a quantum meruit basis.
- **Divisible contracts** - where the contract is in stages, payment can be recovered for the portion of the work that has been completed. It is important to note that an action can lie for failure to complete performance. In Ritchie v Atkinson [1808] 1 KB 219, the court held that the ship owner who had agreed to carry cargo per ton could receive payment for the part of the cargo he carried. However, the ship owner was held liable for failing to carry the entire cargo, in a later action. The divisibility of a contract will always be ascertained from the terms of a contract.
- **Substantial contracts** - This is where the contract is adequately performed but is subject to minor defects and

or omissions, payment should be made for the work that is completed less the cost of remedying the defects and or omissions. Substantial performance is determined as a question of fact. Two cases are worth illustrating here, in Bolton v Mahadeva [1972] 2 All ER 1322, the cost of putting the defects right in a central heating system amounted to one third of the contract price. The Court held that the contract was not substantially performed. However, in Hoenig v Issac [1952] 2 All ER 176, the plaintiff contracted to decorate the Defendants flat and to fir bookcase for the sum of $750.00. The work was completed but had minor defects. The costs to remedy the defects amounted to $50. The Court held that the contract was substantially performed. On the basis of both cases, it would appear that where the costs to remedy the defect is less than one third of the contract price, the contract is likely to be considered substantially performed.

- **Prevention of performance** - Where one party has partly performed the contract and is prevented from completing his own due to the fault of the paying party, the party must be paid for the work he has done on a quantum meruit basis.

2.   Discharge by Agreement

A contract comes into existence by Agreement. In this same manner a contract can come to an end. However, consideration is required to either vary or discharge the Agreement.

3.   Discharge by Breach

According to the words of Treitel, a breach of contract is committed when a party without lawful excuse fails or refuses to perform what is due from them under the contract, or performs defectively or incapacitates themselves from performing. *G.H. Treitel,* The Law of Contract, (Sweet and Maxwell), London, 2003, 832.

4.   Discharge by Frustration

What is Frustration? "Under the doctrine of frustration, a contract can be discharged if, after its formation, but before its performance, events occur making performance of the contract impossible or illegal and in certain analogous situations." *G.H. Treitel,* The Law of Contract, (Sweet and Maxwell), London, 2003, 866. The Courts developed the doctrine of frustration so as to be fair to parties whose failure to perform was beyond their control. If a contract is considered frustrated, it ends at the moment that the intervening event prevented performance.

There are some main classes of situations in which the law will automatically consider the contract frustrated.

- Impossibility
- Change in circumstances
- Subsequent illegality

Impossibility

There are quite a series of events that can happen which will result in the contract becoming frustrated.

1. The Death or other personal incapacity of a party – if a person who has to perform at a concert dies or becomes physically ill, the contract becomes frustrated. This is best illustrated by the case of

Robinson v Davison [1871] LR6 Ex 269, where a pianist became ill and could not perform at a concert. The court held that the contract was frustrated.

2.   The subject matter of the contract becomes destroyed - if the subject matter crucial to the performance of the contract is destroyed, the contract will be frustrated as in Taylor v Caldwell [1863] 32 LJ QB 164. The music hall was hired specifically for the performance of the concert and was accidentally destroyed by fire prior to the concert. The contract was frustrated.

Change in circumstances

Frustration will take place where there is an event which destroys the central purpose of the contract. In Krell v Henry [1903] 2 KB 740, a room was rented for the sole purpose of viewing the coronation procession of King Edward VII from the window of the room. The King became ill and the procession was cancelled and the court held that the contract was frustrated. This case is worth contrasting with Herne Bay steam Boat v Hutton [1903] 2 KB 683, where the Defendant hired a boat to take passengers to view the royal inspection of the fleet that was gathered in the port and to view the fleet itself. The review was cancelled. The Court held that the contract was not frustrated. The court based there decision on the premise that although the purpose of seeing the king was not possible, the Defendant was still able to use the boat to view the fleet. The Court considered that there was still some commercial value in the contract.

Subsequent illegality

A contract that is lawful when made but becomes unlawful before performance takes place as a result of Government action or legislation. Metropolitan Water Board v Dick Kerr & Co [1918] AC 119, the Government delayed the performance of a contract to build a reservoir within 6 years because of the war.

Limitations on the Doctrine of Frustration

The Courts have categorized certain situations in which the doctrine of frustration will not apply

- **Where the frustration is self induced** - where one party is responsible for the event which makes performance impossible, the contract will not be frustrated but the party at fault can be held liable for breach of contract. Maritime National Fish v Ocean Trawlers [1935] AC 524.
- **Onerous contracts** - a contract becomes very difficult to perform due to inflation or labour shortages. Davis Contractors Ltd v Fareham UDC [1956] 2 All ER 145.
- **Undertaking to Perform** - if one party has undertaken to perform his part of the contract, whatever happens he will be liable for breach of contract.
- **Provisions in the contract** - these covered the frustrating event and covered the extent of the loss or damage caused.
- **Leases** - A lease is considered more than a contract in that it is seen as an interest in land and cannot be destroyed.

The Law Reform (FRUSTRATED CONTRACTS) Acts 1943

This Act regulates parties rights whenever frustration arises in the contract and deals with three main areas:

1. Recovery of money paid in advance
2. Recovery of work already completed
3. Recovery for a benefit gained through partial performance

Section 1 (2) of the Law Reform (Frustrated Contracts) Act 1943, provides:

All sums paid or payable to any party in pursuance of the contract before the time when the parties were so discharged shall, in the case of sums paid, be recoverable from him as money received by him for the use of the party by whom the sums were paid, and, in the case of sums so payable, cease to be so payable.

Provided that, if the party to whom the sums were so paid or payable incurred expenses before the time of discharge, or for the purpose of, the performance of the contract, the court may, if it considers it just to do so having regard to all the circumstances of the case, allow him to retain or, as the case may be, recover the whole or any part of the sums so paid or payable, not being an amount in excess of the expenses so incurred.

"This provision confirms the principle that money already paid is recoverable and that money due under the contract ceases to be payable as discussed in Taylor v Caldwell [1863] 3 B&S 826.

Section 1 (3) of the Act considers recovery where a benefit is gained.

"Where any party to the Contract has, by reason of anything done by any other party thereto in, or for the purpose of, the performance of the contract, obtained a valuable benefit before the time of discharge, there shall be recoverable from him by the said other party such sum, not exceeding the value of the said benefit to the party obtaining it, as the court considers just, having regard to all the circumstances of the case and, in particular;-

      a)   The amount of any expenses incurred before the time of discharge by the benefitted party in, or for the purpose of, the performance of the contract, including any sums paid or payable by him to any other party in pursuance of the contract and retained or recoverable by that party under the last foregoing subsection, and

b) The effect, in relation to the said benefit, of the circumstances giving rise to frustration of the contract."

It must be noted as seen in the Act that the court must first consider whether a valuable benefit has been conferred. Once this is established, the court will then consider a sum that is just to award having regard to all the circumstances. In **BP (Libya ltd v Hunt (No.2) [1979] 1 WLR 783**, BP was able to recover $35,000,000 from Hunt after it participated in an oil concession granted to Hunt by the Libyan government and supplied him with oil before the government was overthrown.

Limitations of the Act

The Act specifically excludes certain circumstances as follows:

Section 2 (4) Where the contract is severable and one part has been completely performed. The Courts treat the severable part as if it were separate.

Section 2 (5) (a) Carriage of goods by sea (except time charter parties)

Section 2 (5) (b) Contracts of insurance

Section 2 (5) (c) Perishing of goods under Section 7 of the Sale of Goods Act 1979

Contracts rendered illegal at commonlaw:

- Contracts to promote immorality, Pearce v Brooks [1866] LR 1 Ex 213
- Contracts to commit crime or benefit from the proceeds of crime
- Contracts concerning corruption in public life
- Contracts to impede the course of justice
- Contracts in restraint of trade

Contracts rendered illegal by statute

- Contracts formed for public policy reasons
- Contracts which are formed legally but performed illegally, Hughes v Asset Managers PLC [1995] 3 All ER 669.
- Void ab initio, unenforceable.

A contract which is wholly illegal on formation is void so that no rights or liabilities can arise. It must be noted that any money or property transferred under an illegal contract cannot be recovered in a court action unless the parties are not equally to be blamed. This situation can arise where one party entered into the contract due to force or fraud. In this situation, the innocent party can obtain recovery.

Should a lawfully formed contract be used for an illegal purpose which is known to both parties, the courts will treat the contract as illegal from the onset, Pearce v Brooks [1866] LR 1Ex 213. If one party is unaware of the illegal purpose, then he can enforce the contract, Archbold v Spanglett Ltd [1961] 1 All ER 417.

- standard form contract;
- Section 4: relating to liability for indemnity;

- Section 6 (3) refers to breaches of implied conditions, of Section 13, Section 14 (2) and Section 15 of the Sales of Goods Act 1979.
- Section 8: relating to exclusions for misrepresentation.

Schedule 2 of the Unfair Contract Terms Act: (UCTA)

Section 11 (2) of UCTA refers to schedule 2 of the Act, which provides guidelines of the Application of the reasonableness test as follows:

- The strength of the bargaining positions of the parties.
- Whether the consumer received an inducement to agree to the term.
- Whether the consumer knew or ought reasonably to have known of the existence and extent of the term used.
- Where the term excludes or restricts any relevant liability if some condition was not complied with, whether it was reasonable at the time of the contract to expect that compliance with that condition would be practicable.
- Whether the goods were manufactured, processed or adapted to the special order of the customer.

Section 11 of the UCTA 1977, provides that in relation to the contract term, the requirement of reasonableness... is that the term shall have been a fair and reasonable one to be included having regard to the circumstances which were, or ought reasonably to have been, known to or in the contemplation of the parties when the contract was made.

The Unfair Terms in Consumer Contract Regulations 1999.

The unfair terms in Consumer Contract Regulations 1999 resulted from the EC Directive on Unfair Contract Terms in Consumer

Contracts (93/13/EC) which required member states to ensure that adequate and effective means exist to prevent the continued use of unfair terms in Contracts concluded with customers. The Regulation is narrower than UCTA in the sense that regulations apply to only contracts between business and consumer ie, they do not apply to contracts between businesses. The regulation is wider than UCTA in that it applies to all types of contracts, and it considers the fairness of contracts as a whole and not just the fairness of exclusion clauses.

Chapter 6

Exemption Clauses

Exclusion/Exemption Clauses

Exclusion or Exemption clauses are normally included within a contract to totally exclude or limit a persons or business liability for breach of contract and or negligence. For an exemption clause to be effective at common law, it must be incorporated into the contract, it must be constructed so that it covers the damage and it must be reasonable. Further, there are a number of ways by which exemption clauses are controlled. The first is the common law and secondly, statute has been developed to govern their usage, that is the Unfair Contract Terms Act 1977 (UCTA) and the Unfair Terms in Consumer Contract Regulations 1999. (The Regulations) There are several ways in which a clause can be incorporated within a contract;

By Signing

A clause that is included within a contract that is signed is effective regardless of whether the signee has read the wording and understood, L'Estrange v Graucob [1934] 2 KB 394. In this landmark case a café waitress signed a sales agreement for the purchase of a cigarette vending machine without reading the wording on the document. She was bound by the exclusion clause on the document. Scrutton LJ stated that, when a document containing contractual terms is signed, then, in the absence of fraud, or misrepresentation the party signing it is bound and it is wholly immaterial whether he has read the document or not.

By Notice

Where the exemption clause is an unsigned document, the Claimant is only bound by it if reasonable steps were taken to bring the clause to his attention. A document is contractual if the party to be bound knows that it is intended to have contractual force. In Chapleton v Barry UDC [1940] 1 KB 532, a chair was hired and a ticket was presented to show that the prescribed fee had been paid. It was held that the ticket was just a receipt to acknowledge payment and a reasonable person would not expect to find an exclusion clause on the back of the ticket. However, that is not conclusive to suggest that all tickets with exclusion clauses will be invalid. The courts have held the following documents to have contractual effect; railway ticket (Thompson v LMS Rly [1930] 1 KB 41), a car park ticket (Thornton v Shoe Lane Parking [1971] QB 163). Notice of the clause must be given before or at the time the contract is made and not after. Olley v Marlborough Court Ltd [1949] 1 All ER 127, the Claimant succeeded in her claim for damages after furs were stolen from her hotel room. The exemption clause was brought to her attention after the contract was made.

Course of Dealing

Notice of the exemption clause after the contract is made will be sufficient only if the parties had contracted on a regular basis and the exemption clause was always a part of the contract. Spurling v Bradshaw [1956] 2 All ER 121.

Construction

The Courts role in the construction of exemption clause is to construe the clause to ensure that the clause covers the type of loss and or damage that has occurred. Further, the clause must be clear. The Courts approach to ascertaining the construction of exemption clauses is as follows:

- **Contra Proferentem Rule** - This rule operates such that any ambiguity in the wording of the clause will be construed against the party that is attempting to rely on it. Houghton v Trafalgar Insurance Co [1953] 2 All ER 1409, the Claimant's motor insurance policy provided that the Defendant insurers would not be liable if the vehicle carried an excess load. The Claimant had an accident while carrying six people in a five seater car. The insurance company attempted to rely on the exclusion clause. The Claimant was successful. The Court of Appeal held that the term excess load could mean excess passengers or excess weight and interpreted it as meaning excess weight using a narrow interpretation of load as referring to goods and not to passengers.

- **Fundamental Breach** - The Courts have taken an approach to disallow an exemption clause where there is a breach of contract. However, the House of Lords have rejected this idea of fundamental breach. Photo Production Ltd v Securicor Transport Ltd [1980] AC 827.

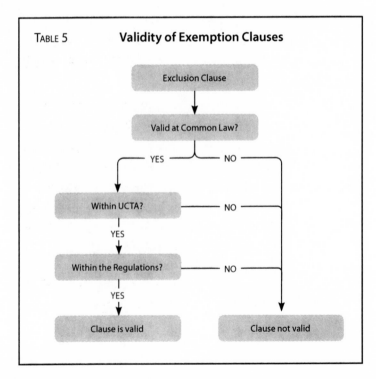

TABLE 5   **Validity of Exemption Clauses**

Reasonableness

The test for reasonableness is contained in the Unfair Contract Terms Act (UCTA) and applies to the following sections:

- Section 2 (2) relating to exclusion of liability for loss other than death or personal injury caused by negligence;
- Section 3: relating to liability for breach of contract, substantially different performance or no performance, where one party deals as consumer or deals on the other's standard form contract;
- Section 4: relating to liability for indemnity;
- Section 6 (3) refers to breaches of implied conditions, 13: 14 (2), 15 of the Sale of Goods Act 1979.
- Section 8: relating to exclusions for misrepresentation.

Unfair Contract Terms Act, (SCHEDULE 2)

Section 11 (2) of UCTA refers to schedule 2 of the Act, which provides guidelines of the Application of the reasonableness test as follows:

- The strength of the bargaining positions of the parties.
- Whether the consumer received an inducement to agree to the term.
- Whether the consumer knew or ought reasonably to have known of the existence and extent of the term used.
- Where the term excludes or restricts any relevant liability if some condition was not complied with, whether it was reasonable at the time of the contract to expect that compliance with that condition would be practicable.
- Whether the goods were manufactured, processed or adapted to the special order of the customer.

Section 11 of the UCTA 1977, provides that in relation to the contract term, the requirement of reasonableness... is that the term shall have been a fair and reasonable one to be included having regard to the circumstances which were, or ought reasonably to have been, known to or in the contemplation of the parties when the contract was made.

The Unfair Terms in Consumer Contract Regulations 1999.

The unfair terms in Consumer Contract Regulations 1999 resulted from the EC Directive on Unfair Contract Terms in Consumer Contracts (93/13/EC) which required member states to ensure that adequate and effective means exist to prevent the continued use of unfair terms in Contracts concluded with customers. The Regulation is narrower than UCTA in the sense that regulations apply to only contracts between business and consumer ie, they do not apply to contracts between businesses. The regulation is wider than UCTA in that it applies to all types of contracts, and it considers the fairness of contracts as a whole and not just the fairness of exclusion clauses.

Unfair Contract Terms Act 1977

Unfair Contract Terms Act (UCTA) generally applies to business liability; Section 1 (3) defines business liability as liability arising from things done or to be done in the course of a business or from the occupation of premises used for business purposes.

Therefore private transactions, (non-business transactions between two private individuals) are not covered by UCTA. The exception to this are as follows:

    1.   Misrepresentation. (Section 8 of UCTA)

2. Implied terms in supply of goods and services contracts. (Section 7 of UCTA)
3. Implied terms in sale of goods and hire-purchase contracts. (Section 6 of UCTA)

Breach Of Contract

Section 3 (2) a of UCTA provides that where one party deals as a consumer or deals on the other's written standard terms of business, then the other party cannot exclude or restrict liability for breach of contract unless the term satisfies the test of reasonableness.

Section 12 (1) of the Act states that a person deals as a consumer if the following criteria is satisfied:

- One party must not make the contract in the course of a business nor hold himself out as doing so; AND
- The other party must make the contract in the course of a business;
- In contracts governed by the law of sale of goods or hire purchase, the goods to which the contract relates must be of a type ordinarily supplied for private use or consumption.
- It should be noted that a consumer can be a natural person or a legal person, ie, a company. R & B Custom Brokers [1988] 1 All ER 847.

Section 12 (2) of the Act provides two examples of instances where a party specifically does not deal as consumer;

- Where the party is not an individual and the goods are sold by auction or competitive tender.
- Where the party is an individual and the goods are secondhand and sold at a private auction.

Negligence

Section 2 (1) of UCTA provides that liability for death or personal injury resulting from negligence cannot be excluded by any contract term or notice.

Section 2 (2) provides that for loss or damage other than personal injury or death, liability may be excluded or limited provided that it satisfies the test of reasonableness.

Chapter 7

Remedies for Breach of Contract

As seen in previous chapters, breach of contract entitles the innocent party to terminate the contract and seek redress in the courts. This Chapter will consider the main remedies that the court can award for breaches of contract and the party that is entitled to the breach.

1. Damages

This is the standard common law remedy for breach of contract and the amount recoverable will be assessed by the courts or can be agreed between the parties in their contractual document. Put simply there are two types of damages, Assessed damages and Agreed damages.

a. Assessed Damages

Assessed Damages is also known as unliquidated damages . Its aim is to compensate the innocent party, who is the Claimant for the financial loss he suffered as a result of the Defendant's breach of the contract. Such loss could encompass expenditure incurred by the Claimant in placing reliance on the contract. It is important to note that in addition to financial loss, the Claimant can also claim for non-financial loss such as physical inconvenience and pain and suffering upon physical injury which are caused by the breach. A category of non-financial loss that is recoverable are damages for mental distress and disappointment unless the purpose of the contract was to provide pleasure and entertainment. Jackson v Horizon Holidays Ltd [1975] 1 WLR 1468.

The Courts make an award by quantifying the losses experienced by the Claimant in money terms. When the loss is one of benefit, the basis of the assessment will be "difference in value" or the "cost of repairs".

b. Agreed Damages

This type of damages is known as liquidated damages. This type of damage is usually written into the contract to avoid the courts applying the complicated principles in unliquidated damages.

2.   Specific Performance

Specific Performance is an equitable remedy that compels the party in breach to fulfill his part of the contract. Specific Performance is positive in nature in that it forces an act to be done. It is not negative in nature such as injunctions which prohibits an act. Specific Performance is only available in one of the following considerations:

- **In situations where damages are not an adequate remedy.**

  In Cohen v Roche [1927] 1 KB 169, the Claimant purchased eight (8) Hellpewhite chairs at an auction and the Defendant refused to honour the sale on the basis that there was an irregularity with the transaction. The Court upheld the validity of the sale but ordered an award of damages rather than specific performance. The courts arrived at their decision on the basis that the chairs were "unremarkable" and possessed no special feature that made them irreplaceable.

  It is worth contrasting this case with Phillis v Lamdin [1949] 2 KB 33 where the Claimant agreed to purchase a house rare door made by Adam. The Defendant delayed the sale and removed the door prior to completion of the sale. The Court held that the door could not be remade or refashioned, therefore the Defendant was told to return the door to its original position in the house.

- **Only available at the discretion of the Judge**

  In Stickney v Keeble [1915] AC 386, that equity will only grant specific performance if under all the circumstances it is just and equitable to do so. A number of principles have been developed from case laws for guidance in this area.

  1. Specific performance will only be granted if other party is willing to perform his side of the bargain.

  2. Specific Performance is not available to the Claimant where he has not provided any consideration.

  3. A Claimant who delays in bringing an action will be denied specific performance. Milward v Earl of Thanet [1801] 5 Ves 720 demonstrates that delay defeats equity.

  4. Walters v Morgan [1861] 2 Cox 369 illustrates the principle that he who comes to equity must come with clean hands. Thus specific performance is not available to a Claimant who behaves dishonestly or improperly.

- **Available for certain types of contract.**

  The general rule is that specific performance will not be ordered in relation to contracts for personal services , such as employment contracts

3. Quantum Meruit

This is classified as compensation where one party cannot complete performance of the contract because of the other party's fault or in instances where partial performance is accepted voluntarily by the other party.

4. Injunction

Injunction is an equitable remedy available to the Courts to restrain the doing of a wrongful act or to compel one party to perform an act.

Limitations on the availability of damages

It is important to bear in mind that there are factors that can limit the availability of damages. These factors are causation, remoteness of damage and mitigation of loss. Let us have a further look on what is involved with these factors.

Causation

A Claimant can recover damages for his loss if the breach of contract is a direct result of his loss. Put simply, the breach must cause the loss. Therefore, if there is an intervening act in the contract and the said intervening act caused the loss, the Claimant cannot recover damages as the chain of causation would have been broken and the loss would not have been a direct result of the breach. In **County Ltd v Girozentrale Securities [1996] 3 All ER, this** case concerns chain of causation and intervening acts, wherein the Claimants bank under wrote 26 million shares in an oil exploration company. The Defendants were engaged by the Claimants in their capacity as stockbrokers to seek investors for the shares. The Defendants acted outside of their agreement in fulfilling their contractual obligation and as a result most of the shares were not sold. The Claimants sought to recover the loss which amounted to £7,000,000. The Court of Appeal upheld the Claimants appeal on the basis that the Defendants had acted outside of their Agreement which caused the Claimants loss.

Remoteness

Having established causation, the second limb to be satisfied is remoteness. The leading case which illustrates remoteness is Hadley v Baxendale [1854] 9 Exch 341. In Hadley, the Claimants suffered losses when their mill was left idle. The court identified 3 categories of losses which are legally recoverable as (a) those losses arising naturally from the breach, this requires no special or expert knowledge, (b) those losses which were in the parties contemplation at the time of the breach, these are special or exceptional losses and requires special knowledge. In Hadley, the courts held that the loss was not an inevitable consequence of the breach since the Defendants could not foresee that their delay would have kept the mill idle. The principles outlined in Hadley were considered in other cases. One such landmark case is Victoria Laundry v Newman [1949] 2 KB 528, wherein the Defendants were held liable for loss of ordinary day to day profits which would have resulted from its use had the boiler been delivered in time, but not for the loss of certain exceptional contracts which the Claimants would have obtained from the Government. The courts in arriving at their decision held that the Defendants knew that the Claimants aimed to increase their business by acquiring another boiler, therefore the loss of additional income was a reasonable foreseeable consequence of the breach.

Chapter 8

Revision

- Examination Tips
- Self Test Questions

Examination Tips

Writing well on Law school exam requires thinking like a Lawyer, and is essential to success at Law school or on the LLB Degree programme. I would best describe excellent writing in Law exams as a specialized art that takes time to practice.

Plan your Response

It is always essential to plan your response- what does this mean?

- Take time to read your questions
- Plan and outline your answers

Doing the above points is time well spent. It will help you to organize your thoughts and also spot additional issues.

Budget your Time

Do not get caught up on challenging questions. In the interest of time, skip a challenging question and move on a question that you are more comfortable in writing the answer. After you have completed the question, you can always revisit the more challenging questions.

Writing answers to essay questions

To write a well organized essay, you should :

- Write clearly and concisely (this will attract points even if you fail to spot an issue)
- Always have an introduction, which should include an outline of the points that you intend to address within the essay. Let the reader be aware of the order in which you intend to address the different points. This will

create a point of direction for the reader and will attract an extra point.

- Always include the rule of law that governs a particular issue and analyse the rule of law in relation to the facts.
- Professor's job will be much easier in writing a well organized essay.

Review Past exam papers:

Many Professors maintain a file of past exam papers. Most likely, questions are taken from this pool of past exam questions. It is always helpful to brainstorm answers with other students. Past papers also gives flavor of exam style and format.

IRAC

A successful approach which I have used throughout law school and have advocated to my students is IRAC. This stands for Issue, rule analysis and conclusion. This is particularly useful for problem solving questions and can easily be adopted for essay questions too.

I   Issue - always spot the *issue* in the question.

R   Rule - state the *rule* of law that governs the particular issue.

A   Apply - *apply* the particular facts to the rule and analyse the situation. Always use case laws and or statute to support your reasoning. It is always best to argue both sides.

C   Conclusion - end your answer with a *conclusion*. In other words tell the marker your advise to the situation and the reason for that particular advise.

Always

1. Use key case laws to illustrate your answer and to support your reasoning.
2. Recall key principles from the case laws that you have used.
3. Test your ability to answer questions by planning out answers to revision questions.
4. Follow up with further reading to ensure that you are comfortable in attempting to write the essay questions.

Self Test Questions

1. Can liability be excluded for misrepresentation?
2. What is the effect of misrepresentation on a Contract?
3. What are the main differences between negligent and innocent misrepresentation?
4. On what basis are damages assessed under Section 2 (1) of the Misrepresentation Act 1967?
5. Explain how you can be liable for misrepresentation if the statement you made is true.

Tom advertises a racehorse, Gallop for sale in the local papers. In the advertisement, Tom stated that the horse can be inspected at his stables in Newport. Tub arranges to go and see the horse, and takes with him a friend, Leroy, who is a racehorse trainer and has adequate knowledge about horses.

Tub and Leroy inspects Gallop. Tub asks about Gallops pedigree and Tom offered to get the pedigree documents from his office, but Tub says it was not necessary. Leroy stated to Tub that he thinks Gallop has great potential.

A month later Tub made a decision to purchase Gallop. He has had it for two weeks preceding the month, during which time it ran is several races without any success. After the purchase, Gallop ran in all six races for which it entered and came last in all.

Tub is upset and decides to take up the matter with Tom. Advise Tub.

1. Define offer
2. What is an invitation to treat?
3. What is the distinction between and offer and an invitation to treat?

4.   Define acceptance

5.   In what circumstances does the postal rule apply?

6.   Explain the general rule concerning communication of acceptance

7.   In what ways can an offer be terminated

8.   What constitutes a rejection of an offer?

9.   How do we terminate an offer?

On 25th October, Susan, a newly qualified Dentist, receives the following note from her Uncle:

14 Park Lane

Manchester, Jamaica.

Dear Susan,

Further to our telephone conversation about you buying some of my dental equipment. I am now prepared to let you have everything for a total sum of $20,000. Let me know as soon as possible as I have another offer from a dear friend.

Susan is very keen to take advantage of her Uncle's offer but does not know how she will raise the money by ending of October. She telephone her Uncle to find out whether she can have until end of December to pay. Her Uncle is not at home so Susan left a message with his Secretary. Two weeks has passed and Susan did not hear from her Uncle so she went to her local bank and arranged a loan. On 25th November, Susan writes to her Uncle accepting his offer and enclosed a Managers cheque in the sum of $20,000. On the 31st November Susan receives a telephone call from her Uncle informing her that he has already sold the equipment to someone else. Advise Susan.

1. What are exemptions clauses?
2. Explain how exemption clauses clauses can be incorporated into a Contract.
3. Who bears the burden of proving that an exemption clause satisfies the requirement of reasonableness?
4. What is business liability?
5. Which Contracts are excluded from the scope of Unfair Contract Terms Act 1977?

Gary buys second hand vehicles, repairs them and sells them. He always displays a notice at the entrance of his business premises stating that they are second hand and are bought at the purchaser's risk. Members of the public buy some of these vehicles and car dealers.

Gary uses faulty inferior materials to repair these vehicles. Dian buys one of the car from Gary. He pays for the car by credit card. Two days after the purchase Dian was driving the car to work when the engine ignites and starts a fire. Dian suffers burn when she tries to put the fire out. Dian recently learned that Gary is in financial difficulties and may cease trading. Advise Gary of any liability on his part.

Leabharlanna Poibli Chathair Bhaile Átha Cliath
Dublin City Public Libraries

CPSIA information can be obtained at www.ICGtesting.com
Printed in the USA
LVOW07s1720181016

509270LV00001B/16/P

9 781504 905558